IMAGES
of America

HOOSIER
HIGH SCHOOL
BASKETBALL

This old basketball goal is on the grounds of the former Booker T. Washington School in Rushville. Black students in Rushville went to this school until they began high school. (Photo by Bob Adams.)

Front Cover: The Mauckport High School "Pilots" never had a gym, and played on the outdoor court where this picture was taken. Cheerleaders are (from left to right): Alice Jacobs, Helen Singleton, and Nina Faith Beanblossom. Team members were (second row) Rex Bliss, Coach Marlin McCoy, Lamar Smith, Verelle Mackison, Herschel Frakes, Bobby Scott (team manager), and Paul Singleton. In the back row are: Arthur Ray Timberlake, Darrell Jacobs, Kermit Hays, Hugh "Sonny" Foster, and Harold McBride. (Photo supplied by Nina Faith Beanblossom.)

IMAGES
of America

HOOSIER
HIGH SCHOOL
BASKETBALL

Bob Adams

ARCADIA
PUBLISHING

Published by Arcadia Publishing
Charleston, South Carolina

Library of Congress Catalog Card Number: 2002104608

For all general information contact Arcadia Publishing at:
Telephone 843-853-2070
Fax 843-853-0044
E-mail sales@arcadiapublishing.com
For customer service and orders:
Toll-Free 1-888-313-2665

Visit us on the Internet at www.arcadiapublishing.com

The last of the Norsemen. This was the last team at Eaton High School, which closed at the end of the 1966-67 school year and consolidated with Royerton and DeSoto to form Delta High School. The last Norsemen were: (from left to right) Larry Wilson, Dennis Lewman, Dan Reagan, Gary Brennaman, Homer Fruit, Coach Loren Skinner, Rick Johnson, Bill Mickler, Dan Cooper, and Doyle Reagan. Kneeling were Rick Atchley and Bob McAmis.

CONTENTS

ACKNOWLEDGMENTS

First of all, I have to thank my wife Terri, who spent endless hours by my side as we traversed the state looking for, and taking pictures of, the many old high school teams, gyms, and buildings in this book.

I would also like to thank Pleasant Mills grad Olin Edgell for letting me use his vast yearbook collection. Thanks also go to Wendell Trogdon, Clint Anderson, Dean Monroe, Greg Alexander, Deb Eidson, Bob Whalen, Wawasee girls' Coach Kem Zolman, and Shane Frost for supplying me with some of the pictures in the book. Thanks also go out to the Decatur Library, the Berne Library, and the Adams County Historical Society for helping me locate materials.

This book is dedicated to my wife Terri, who has put up with my obsession with Indiana High School basketball. It is also dedicated to my father, who was always my biggest fan, and to my two grandchildren, Madalyn and McKinley, who, along with their parents, have brought indescribable joy to my life.

INTRODUCTION

Dr. James Naismith invented the game of basketball while teaching at Springfield College in 1891. Springfield College was the training ground for YMCA secretaries. Naismith invented the game as a way to keep these young men in shape during the winter.

One of these young men was the Reverend Nicholas McKay. He was sent to Crawfordsville upon completing his studies at Springfield College, and he took the game with him. The first game in the state was believed to have been played in 1894, and pitted the Crawfordsville YMCA team against the team from the Lafayette YMCA. It was reported that each team played nine men at a time.

The girls got involved with the game early, also. By 1898, the Indianapolis High School (later Shortridge) girls had played the Knickerbocker Hall girls. As a matter of fact, boys at many schools in the early years refused to play the game because it was considered "sissy."

Former Indiana coach Bob Knight is credited with the saying, "Basketball may have been invented in Massachusetts, but it was made for Indiana." The game quickly spread to the many small high schools that dotted the Hoosier landscape. When the Indiana University Athletic Boosters hosted the first state tourney in 1911, only 12 teams were involved. This quickly grew, and by 1938 over 800 schools entered tourney play.

The so-called "Golden Age" of Indiana high school basketball began after World War II and probably ended in 1990. During these years, many small schools, such as Chester Township of Wabash County, Silver Lake, Jefferson Township of Randolph County, and Berne reached the "Sweet 16." Small schools reached the summit in 1954 when tiny Milan upset perennial state-power Muncie Central in the state finals, 32-30. This game made household names out of Coach Marvin Wood and Milan player Bobby Plump, who hit "the shot heard round the world."

Many towns built large gyms to take advantage of the popularity of the sport. Many places, like Huntingburg, built arenas large enough to hold more than the population of the entire town in hopes of hosting a sectional.

School consolidation, which started in the late 1940s, began cutting into attendance at ballgames. By the late 1960s, the number of high schools entered in the state tourney had shrunk to under 400. But, thanks to players like Oscar Robertson, Jimmy Rayl, Ron Bonham, George McGinnis, Kyle Macy, and Scott Skiles, attendance at ballgames remained strong.

This culminated in 1990 when Damon Bailey led his Bedford-North Lawrence Stars to a state championship in front of 40,000 fans at the Hoosier (now RCA) Dome in Indianapolis.

Basketball, which had been the only game in town in the 1940s and 1950s, now had to compete with other sports such as wrestling and swimming for fans. As other avenues of entertainment opened up, attendance at games dropped even further. The change from a single-class to a multi-class format continues to eat into the fan base.

But none of the attendance problems of the past decade can take anything away from the glory, the splendor, and the experience of almost a century of Indiana high school basketball.

Decatur, Indiana
March 12, 2002

One

THE PIONEERS

Springfield College was founded in 1885 by D.A. Reed to train YMCA secretaries. It was here that James Naismith invented basketball in December of 1891. (Photo from the collection of Bob Adams.)

James Naismith (1861-1939) was born in Ontario, Canada. He graduated from McGill University in Montreal in 1877. He attended the two-year YMCA course at Springfield, but was made an instructor after completing the first year. At the request of physical education director Luther Gulick, Naismith designed a game to keep athletes in shape during the winter. Naismith's list of 13 original rules were typed up on two pages and tacked to a bulletin board in the gym. (Photo from the collection of Bob Adams.)

Y. M. C. A. Building, Crawfordsville, Ind.

It was here, at the YMCA in Crawfordsville, Indiana, that the Reverend Nicholas McKay introduced the game in 1893. In March of 1894, the Crawfordsville YMCA beat the Lafayette YMCA, 45-21. (Photo from the collection of Bob Adams.)

A.R. Huyette was the principal at Keystone High School in 1898 when he introduced the game of basketball in Wells County. He was later the Wells County School Superintendent. (Photo from the collection of Bob Adams.)

The outside basketball court at Keystone High School consisted of two peach baskets nailed to two trees about 100 feet apart. Another tree grew near the center of the "court." (Photo from the collection of Bob Adams.)

11

Ken Kiser played basketball at Keystone and graduated in 1901. He introduced the game at Berne High School in 1903. The first game between two Adams County schools was played in 1906 when Decatur defeated Berne, 9-6. (Photo courtesy of the Berne Library.)

By 1906, basketball had spread to Williamsport High School. Note the heavy uniforms worn by these players to protect themselves while playing on outside courts made of gravel and cinders. (Photo from the collection of Bob Adams.)

This 1908 Ladoga team consisted of Simmons, Meyers, and Cox at forward, Cline and Cave at center, and Price, Rapp, and Bachelder at guard. They won 10 of 13 games played. (Photo from the collection of Bob Adams.)

This team from Crawfordsville won the first state tourney in 1911. It was held on the campus of Indiana University, and was hosted by the IU Booster Club. It was an invitation-only tourney, with one team from each of Indiana's congressional districts invited to play. The Indianapolis School Board would not let Shortridge attend, so only 12 teams competed for the title. The Crawfordsville team was made up of Orville Taylor, Carroll Stevenson, Hugh Miller, Ben Myers, T. Newton Hill, Cleo Shaw, and Grady Chadwick. Dave Glascock was the coach. Stevenson led the team in scoring with 14 points. It wasn't until 1957 that the Indiana High School Athletic Association officially recognized this team as the first state champs. (Photo courtesy of Bob Whalen.)

This building on the campus of Indiana University was the home of the first state tourney. (Photo from the collection of Bob Adams.)

Even though this 1912 Decatur team won 10 of 12 games, they were not invited to play in the state tourney. The organizers of the state tourney, which was started in 1911, invited one team from each of the state's congressional districts. Team members were, from left to right: (front row) Cy Vancil Robert Peterson, and Dan Tyndall; (back row) Sherman Beery, Frank Lose, Kenneth Vancil, Joe McConnell, and Coach Martin Worthman. (Photo from the yearbook collection of Olin Edgell.)

14

Max Beigh coached this 1938 Kirkland Township team to a runner-up spot in the Adams County Tourney. Team members were, from left to right: (standing) Hansel Foley, principal, Paul Baumgartner, Art Girod, Bob Presdorf, Luther Engle, Carl Arnold, Dale Baumgartner, Dwight Arnold, Dick Gerber, and Coach Max Beigh; (sitting) Dean Runkel, Chalmer Borne-student manager, and Sylvan Ringger. (Photo courtesy of the Adams County Historical Society.)

This 1948 Monroeville team won the Allen County Athletic tourney, and then became the first Allen County school (outside of Fort Wayne) to win a Fort Wayne Sectional. The team also won a regional title before losing to Muncie Central in the Semi-State. Team members were, from left to right: (sitting) James Miller-student manager, Stanley Shaffer, Max Brown, Robert Hullinger, and Eugene Rhodes; (standing) George Martin-principal, Donald Lehrman, Merritt Myers, Roland (Abner) Lee, Richard Reinking, Byrnon (Newt) Beucler, and Coach William Milliner. (Photo supplied by Deb Eidson.)

15

50 Years later, in June of 1998, the Monroeville team got together for a reunion. Sitting from left to right are: (front row) Max Hill (mascot), Byron (Newt) Beucler, Eugene Rhodes, Coach Bill Milliner, Stanley Shaffer, Merritt Myers, and Donald Lehrman; (standing in the back row) Richard Reinking, Max Brown, Paul Lortie, Lynn Bearman, Glen Lehrman, James Giant, Gordon Wolff (cheerleader), and Marvin Smith (cheerleader).

Members of this 1912 Oaktown team are, from left to right: (front row) Clyde Fox, Raymond Sproat, Barney Orndorff, and Lester Maynard; (middle row) Bryce Bond; (back row) Gilbert Walker, Coach Sartor, and Clyde McCord. This team won twice in seven games and played home and home series with Wheatland, Decker, and Freelandville. They also played Bruceville once. (Photo from the yearbook collection of Olin Edgell.)

16

Players making up this 1912 Lagro team were, from left to right: (front row) Herm Schamlzried, Harry Williams, Wilbur Baer, Leo Cleveland, and Forest Porter; (back row) Unknown, Carl Bonewit-coach and principal, and unknown. (Photo from the yearbook collection of Bob Adams.)

Walter Carnahan coached this 1914 Frichton team. Team members were (left to right): Carnahan, Lee Reel, Hiram Mallory, Clarence Welton, Maurice Wilson, Ralph Welton, and Earl McClure. (Photo from the yearbook collection of Bob Adams.)

This 1935 Berne team, coached by Judson Erne, went all the way to the 16-team state finals where they beat Roachdale before falling to Shelbyville. Eight years later, Herman Neunschwander (#11) was the coach at Monroe, where his Bearkatz won a sectional and regional title before losing in the Semi-State. Bob Dro (#86), played for Branch McCracken at IU and was a member of the school's first NCAA championship team in 1940. Jerome Steiner (#33), played for Tony Hinkle at Butler. Steiner, who also became a high school coach, was better known as a referee. Steiner and Dro were both elected to the Indiana Basketball Hall of Fame. Other team members were Gordon Felber, Arnold Fluekiger, Ed Stuckey, Elmer Winteregg Jr., Les Habegger, Robert Parrish, and Clair Sprunger.

D.C. Graham coached the Marengo Cavemen in 1934. Team members were, from left to right: (front) H.O. Jones, Bill Wyman, Grant Pavey, Lowell Nicholson, Robert Ross, and Superintendent O.M. Sheckells; (back row) Coach D.C. Graham, Paul Van Meter, Arthur Weathers, Leon Lambdin, Merl Haycox, and J. Jones. (Photo courtesy of Mrs. Norman Beals.)

Monroe (Adams County) had fielded a boys' basketball team as early as 1910. Clyde Hendricks coached this 1916 version. Team members were, from left to right, Art Spuller, Clarence Elzey, Don Andrews, Cecil Rickord, Chelsie Strait, Ray Crist, Dan Adler, and Ralph Stodhill. (Photo courtesy Adams County Historical Society.)

By 1918, the Monroe team had traded their Sunday best for basketball uniforms. Team members were, from left to right, W. Oliver, Ray Crist, Ray Spuller, Harve Haggard, John Shirk, Ray Keller, and Otis Meyer. Clyde Hendricks coached the team. Harve Haggard went on to become a coach and a long-time educator in Adams County. The sign reads: Monroe Basketball Team 1918. America Forever. (Photo from the photo collection of Bob Adams.)

This 1920 Swayzee team won just seven games in 23 attempts and lost to Kokomo in the opening round of the sectional. From left to right are: (front row) Cecil Symons, Wayne Hite, and Coach E.L. Tierney; (back row) Ralph Peterson, Jean Loy, Harold Spears, and Wayne Hardesty. (Photo from the yearbook collection of Olin Edgell.)

Dale Nussbaum, Harold Reynolds, Daniel Hoffman, Loyal Liddy, and Robert Shoemaker took to the court for Hartford Township (Adams County) in 1921. (Photo from the yearbook collection of Olin Edgell.)

20

Members of this 1922 Decker freshmen team included Edson Catt, who was the long-time coach and principal at Decker Chapel; Don Davis, who coached at Decker, Monroe City, Pekin, Odin, and Mt. Olympus; Frank Dick, who was the long-time principal at Decker; Don Palmer, who coached and taught at Decker for over 40 years; and Earl Palmer, who was a long-time teacher at Southport. (Photo from the yearbook collection of Olin Edgell.)

Honey Creek in Vigo County was the home of the "Honey Bees." This team was coached by Harry Dowell and team members were Morgan, Beall, Farmer, Whitlock, Fox, Grace, and Sipson. (Photo from the collection of Bob Adams.)

Principal John Wayne coached the 1922 Monroeville Cubs. Team members were, from left to right: (front row) Maurice Castleman, Asa Brower, and Howard Savieo; (back row) Carl Reynolds, Cecil Troyer, Cliff Rich, and Ted Brouwer. (Photo courtesy of Deb Eidson.)

Members of the 1923 Plainfield team were Albert Pike, Russell Copeland, Paul Franklin, Roy Jackson, Fay Morrisson, Dot Copeland, Harold Jacks, and Hildreth Glenn. (Photo from the yearbook collection of Olin Edgell.)

This 1924 Van Buren Township (Clay County) team was coached by Albert Mauer. Team members were John Teany, Siebert Slack, James Curley, Thomas Price, Bill Cash, Jenkins, Kenneth Marshall, and Robert Dowan. They won 11 of 19 games. (Photo from the yearbook collection of Bob Adams.)

This 1927 Waldron team won the Shelby County tourney and had a 20-game winning streak. Team members were George Cuskaden, Lawrence Craig, Norman Kanouse, Leonard Miller, Louis Niebert, Malcolm Clay, Ralph Lux, Bernard Miller, Roy Yeager, and Maurice Clay. (Photo from the yearbook collection of Bob Adams.)

These young men represented Fort Branch during the 1926-27 season. (Photo from the yearbook collection of Bob Adams.)

This 1928 Eaton team, coached by Bedford Butcher, lost its second game of the season and its last game of the season to eventual state champ Muncie Central. In between, it won 27 straight games to finish the season 28-2. (Photo from the collection of Bob Adams.)

24

Enoch Troth, Odean Dickey, James Meadgerlein, George Blari, Joy Sindlinger, Boyd Fulk, and George Fulk represented Patricksburg in 1929. Cletus Jenkins was the team coach. (Photo from the yearbook collection of Bob Adams.)

Even though the date on the ball says 1948-49, this is actually a picture of the 1949-50 team at Mauckport, which was the last team in school history. The school closed at the end of that school year and the students went to Corydon High School. The front row consists of cheerleaders Donna Lopp, Mary Ann Goldman, and Darlene Frakes, and Jimmy North, the team manager. Standing in the back row are Farrell Wayne Duley, Wayne Jacobs, Clinton Fisher, Rex Blixx, Norman Timberlake, Paul Singleton, Arthur Ray Timerlake, Darrell Jacobs, Harold McBride, and Lamar Smith. (Photo supplied by Nina Faith Beanblossom.)

The 1922-23 season was just the second season for this Decatur Catholic team. Their coach, Lawrence "Lank" Linn, had just graduated from Decatur High School the previous year. Team members were, from left to right; (front row) Art Voglewede, Earl Christian, Father Peters, Lawrence Linn-coach, Hugh Holthouse, and George Laurent; (back row) Fred Schulte, Art Wemhoff, Andy Appleman, Bob Voglewede, Al Schneider, Carl Gass, Mickey Mylott, and "Mongo" Meyers. Meyers would go on to play at Notre Dame while Laurent would return to coach the Commodores to a Catholic State Championship in 1930.

This 1958-59 Decatur High School team was the last sectional winner from the school. Decatur closed following the 1966-67 school year and consolidated with Monmouth and Decatur Catholic to become Bellmont. Kneeling are Yellow Jackets Denny Bollenbacher, John Cowan, and Tom Grabill. Standing are Jim Reidenbach, Bill Bischoff, Larry Daniels, Bob Shraluka, Bob Fraughiger, Larry Hill, Jim Gay, John Foor, and Richard Canales.

26

This 1961 Pleasant Mills team was 0-15 on the season when they called on the Gray Redbirds. Gray was in the midst of a 32 game losing streak. In a game called the "Zero Bowl," it was rumored that Gray coach Jerry Bailey had scouted Pleasant Mills seven times and the refs in the game were Bailey's college roommate and the best man at his wedding. Gray won 62-50. Pleasant Mills won their first and only game of the season a couple of weeks later when they beat Topeka. Gray and Pleasant Mills both closed at the end of the 1963 school year. Pleasant Mills team members were Jerry Smith, Jim Death, David Currie, David Myers, Bob Martz, Roger Beer, Ronnie Daniels, Marvin Luginbill, Richard Luginbill, Larry Burkhart, and Melvin Ohler.

The 1932 team at Clayton was made up of Alton Franklin, Richard Nicholson, Glen Thompson, Frank Walton, Carl Burns, Raymond Parks, Herman Franklin, Marion Short, Wayne Mynatt, Hilden Tharp, Wayne Wingler, Jewell Michael, Donald Ruston, and Ross Mitchell. A Mr. Fisher was listed as coach. (Photo from the yearbook collection of Olin Edgell.)

This 1935 Stinesville team carried the nickname of "Quarry Lads" after the limestone that was quarried nearby. The Stinesville School, pictured below was made from locally quarried limestone. (Photo from the yearbook collection of Olin Edgell.)

Stinesville High School. (Photo from the yearbook collection of Olin Edgell.)

Arcadia High School in Hamilton County was home to this team in 1936. (Photo from the yearbook collection of Olin Edgell.)

These young men represented Tangier in Parke County during the 1937-38 season. Note the uniform numbers. Numbers higher than five are no longer allowed. (Photo from the yearbook collection of Olin Edgell.)

The 1939 Lagro team, from left to right: D.D. Berry, Ed Fulton, Dick Thomas, Bud Goebel, Bill Hollenback, Dwayne Burcroff, Bob Carpenter, Wayne Crit, Jack Slusser, Orville Brothers, and Ed Wright. At the beginning of the 1938-39 season, Paul Bartholomew was the head coach and principal at Lagro. He was shot by another teacher on November 11, 1938, and died the next day. Lagro had played and lost to Linlawn on November 11. Bartholomew was a 1913 Lagro graduate. (Photo from the yearbook collection of Olin Edgell.)

The Pleasant Mills Spartans dedicated their new gym during the 1939-40 season, and then went on to win a sectional title for the first time. Prior to the 1940 sectional, Pleasant Mills had never even won a sectional game. This team beat Hartford Township, Berne, and Monroe to win the sectional title, but fell to Mentone in the opening game of the regional, and finished the season with a 21-6 record. (Photo from the yearbook collection of Olin Edgell.)

Walton won the Cass County Tourney in 1930 by beating Galveston, New Waverly, Young America, and Lucerne. The team was consisted of Bud Cotner, Punk Phillips, Boone Ballard, Rudy Hyman, Doc Fitzer, Jim Hall, Kip Layman, Paul Rush, and Jake Betzner. P.G. Hoffner was the coach.

Deane Moore, Loen Mossburg, Roger Shaw, Bernard Fiedler, Mike Garrett, Dick Coolman, Pat Garrett, Jim Schneider, Ray Clark, and Joe Moore played for Coach Ernest Curtis at Liberty Center in 1942. (Photo from the yearbook collection of Olin Edgell.)

Rolland Van Skoyoc coached this 1944 Williamsport team. Players on the team were Tom Flesher, Dale Beckett, Bill Carlson, Donald Wallace, Charles Johnson, Don Slauter, Jim Kane, and Homer Aldridge. (Photo from the yearbook collection of Olin Edgell.)

Coach Gerald Vizard (second from left-top row) was the coach when Pleasant Mill won their second and last sectional in 1942. Harold Sapp (fourth from left-top row) later would become the mascot of the Bellmont Braves and Squaws and would attend Bellmont games dressed in traditional Indian garb. Harold August (sixth from left-top row) would later become Adams County Sheriff. Principal Olen Marsh (next to last-right side-top row) had coached at Jackson Township (Randolph County), Jefferson Township (Adams County), and Parker City. He was principal at several Adams County schools, and was a son of the founder of Marsh Supermarkets. (Photo from the yearbook collection of Olin Edgell.)

Two

THE GIRLS PLAYED TOO

Girls started playing in the state before the turn of the century. By the time the depression was in full swing, girls' basketball had vanished at most schools. Many schools did not have reserve teams, and the girls' games became the opening act for the boys' games.

Early on, some schools had girls' teams but not boys', because basketball, in the early days, was considered by many to be a "sissy" sport.

The 1913 Frichton girls in action during the 1912-13 season. Team members were Lucia Cruft Culbertson, Avis Powell Burnett, Sall Rogers, Elsie Williams, Carrie Mack Kensler, Bertha Dreiman McClure, and Harriet Daines. They were coached by Ethel Campbell. (Photo from the yearbook collection of Olin Edgell.)

Indianapolis High School (later Shortridge) had one of the first girls' teams in the state during the 1898-99 school year. (From the collection of Bob Adams.)

/397. German House, Indianapolis, Ind.

The girls from Indianapolis High School and the German House girls played a game here during the 1900-1901 school season. (From the collection of Bob Adams.)

These girls took to the court for Ladoga High School in 1908. (Photo from the yearbook collection of Olin Edgell.)

Lucia Craft Culbertson, Carrie Mack Kensler, Tess Wilson, Bertha Dreiman McClure, and Elsie Williams all smiled for the camera. They played for Frichton during the 1910-11 school year. (Photo from the yearbook collection of Olin Edgell.)

Sailor shirts and bloomers were the order of the day for the Swayzee girls in 1920. Team members were Faye Henderson, Esther Johnson, Effie Collins, Maurine Groscost, Ada Black, Anna Parson, and Delight Collins. Miss Prall coached the team to a 1-0-1 record. They played two games with Sharpsville, winning one game 2-0, and fighting to a scoreless tie in the other. (Photo from the yearbook collection of Olin Edgell.)

The 1921-22 Decatur girls won thirteen straight games to finish the season undefeated. They also laid claim to a mythical state championship. This team lost only three games in three seasons. Team members were Melvena Butler, Margaret Moran, Bee Peterson, Germain Christian, Mildred Leonard, Ella Worthman, Crystal Baltzell, Margaret Zwick, Margaret Lankenau, and Marcella Hower. (Photo from the yearbook collection of Olin Edgell.)

The 1927-28 season was the first for the girls at Eaton High School. The girls split two games. (From the collection of Bob Adams.)

Playing for Coach Jeanette Clark and the Decatur Yellow Jackets in 1929, from left to right, were Iverana Werling, Florence Anderson, Osie Smith, Helen Moseschberger, Louise Mann, Margaret Martin, Evelyn Grunden, Martha Noll, and Ina Anderson. Seated is Cleo Werling,

The 1929 Culver Girls Team members were Margaret McCullough, Velda Warner, Wilmetta Dykes, Jean Scott, Lavin Newman, Opal Crump, Jeanette Stevens, Mary Riggens, Mis Buar, Ann Jane McClane, and Ruth Newman. (Photo from the yearbook collection of Olin Edgell.)

The 1932 Clayton Girls, from left to right: Thelma Sawyer, Mary Scott, Margaret Wright, Bertha Reeves, Crystal Mason, LaDonna Sears, Louanna Thompson, Kathleen Littell, Eva Walton, Nathalie Mabe, Rosaleen Barnes, Charlotte Havens, and Laura Marie Richards. Most of the girls' teams disbanded before World War II. Many schools played Girls' Athletics in the 1950s and 1960s. The IHSAA sanctioned girls' basketball in 1975 and the girls played in their first state tourney in 1976. (Photo from the yearbook collection of Olin Edgell.)

38

Three

THEY COACHED THE GAME

Bedford Butcher was a graduate of Pennville High School. He later returned to coach at that school. He also coached at Eaton and Winchester. In three years at Eaton, his teams won over 70 games and also won the first Delaware County tourney championship in 1929. (Photo from the collection of Bob Adams.)

Glen Harper coached at New Ross, Noblesville, Hagerstown, and Twin Lakes. His teams won 9 sectionals and 3 regional titles. His 1956 New Ross team put together an undefeated season and won a sectional and regional title. (Photo from the yearbook collection of Olin Edgell.)

Clyde Hendricks coached at Monroe from 1915-1925. He took his 1921 team to the 16-team state finals. When the citizens of the town of Monroe refused to build a community building for the school to use as a gym, Hendricks suspended basketball at the school for a season. His 1921 team beat Berne, 142-2. (Photo from the yearbook collection of Olin Edgell.)

P.G. "Mike" Hoffer coached Walton to a Cass County Championship in 1930. He was a graduate of Anderson High School and Muncie Normal. (Photo from the yearbook collection of Olin Edgell.)

Earl Snider won over 400 games while coaching Franklin Township, Selma, Yorktown, and Daleville. His teams also won five Delaware County championships. (Photo from the yearbook collection of Olin Edgell.)

Harold Schutz won 294 games and four sectional titles while coaching at Etna Green, Geneva, and Portland. He was later the long time athletic director at Portland and Jay County.

Chet Francis won 130 games in 10 seasons (1948-1957) while coaching the Vincennes Alices. He passed away in 2002. (Photo from the yearbook collection of Olin Edgell.)

Herb Curtis was Branch McCracken's high school coach at Monrovia. McCracken went on to coach at Ball State and Indiana University, where his Hoosier teams won two NCAA titles. Curtis's teams at Monrovia and Decatur won about 250 games and 3 sectional titles in 10 seasons. He made the move from Monrovia to Decatur after his Monrovia teams couldn't get by Martinsville in the sectional. The Artesians were coached by Herb's older brother, Glenn. (Photo from the yearbook collection of Olin Edgell.)

Glenn Curtis won over 500 games as a coach at Lebanon, Rushville, Martinsville, and Indiana State. He won a state championship with Lebanon in 1918, his first season as a head coach. He was John Wooden's high school coach at Martinsville. Wooden followed Curtis at Indiana State before moving on to UCLA, where he won 10 NCAA championships. Curtis went on to coach three more state championship teams at Martinsville before taking the Indiana State job. He was elected to the Indiana High School Basketball Hall of Fame in 1962. (Photo from the collection of Bob Adams.)

Ernest Curtis, a cousin to Herb and Glenn Curtis, was the head basketball coach of at least 14 different schools. His coaching career included stops at Guilford, Leesburg, Kniman, Linlawn, Boone Grove, Scotland, Cuzco, Sanborn, Monmouth, Owensburg, Griffin, Liberty Center, Clifford, and Kingsbury. (Photo from the yearbook collection of Olin Edgell.)

Cletus Jenkins had a 16-year coaching career that included stints at Patricksburg, Quincy, Oolitic, and Butler. (Photo from the yearbook collection of Olin Edgell.)

44

Don Walker "Pappy" coached at Decker High School in Knox County in some capacity for over 40 years. (From the yearbook collection of Bob Adams.)

Bill Berberian won over 400 games while coaching at Greensburg and West Lafayette. His 31-year coaching career included 28 seasons at West Lafayette. (Photo from the yearbook collection of Olin Edgell.)

Martin Worthman took two early Decatur teams to the state finals. His 1913 team lost to South Bend and his 1914 team lost to Rochester. He later became Superintendent of the Decatur Schools. His son, Robert, would coach basketball and football at Decatur in the late 1940s and 1950s. (Photo from the yearbook collection of Olin Edgell.)

Harold Anson had a 20-year coaching career at Albany, Batesville, Crawfordsville, Silver Creek, and Boonville. A graduate of Ball State, his teams won four sectional championships. (Photo from the yearbook collection of Olin Edgell.)

Robert Scott coached at Lewisville for 11 seasons and ended up winning 176 games. His star player for four of those seasons was Marion Pierce, who became the first player in the state to surpass 3,000 career points. (Photo from the yearbook collection of Olin Edgell.)

Jack Butcher has won more games than any other coach in the state. He has coached at Loogootee for 45 years and by the end of the 2001-2002 season his Lion teams had won 806 ball games. (Photo by Bob Adams.)

In a career that spanned 46 seasons, and included stops at Clinton Township, Monon, Honey Creek, Terre Haute Gerstmeyer, Terre Haute North, and North Knox, Howard Sharpe-coached-teams won more than 700 ballgames. (Photo from the yearbook collection of Olin Edgell.)

Gerald Vizard had a varied career. In addition to coaching at Pleasant Mills and Decatur Catholic, he also worked at General Electric and once owned a Studebaker dealership. (Photo from the yearbook collection of Olin Edgell.)

J.O. Fortner coached for 16 seasons at Russiaville, Rockport, Bloomingdale, and Concannon. (Photo from the yearbook collection of Olin Edgell.)

Harry Anderson's teams at Stoney Creek, Ridgeville, and
Geneva won 110 games in 11 seasons. Anderson was later the
long-time Athletic Director at South Adams High School.
(Photo from the yearbook collection of Olin Edgell.)

Herman Hinshaw was a graduate of
Lapel. He returned to coach at the
school and led the Bulldogs to a final
four spot in the 1940 tourney. In 1952,
his team at Indianapolis Tech was
runner-up to Muncie Central. (Photo
from the yearbook collection of
Olin Edgell.)

Maurice Kennedy coached at seven different schools, and won sectional titles with three of them. He took his 1930 Terre Haute Wiley team all the way to the final four and they finished the season with a 30-6 record. He also won sectionals at Winchester and Hartford City. His career also included coaching stops at Washington Township (Clinton County), Decatur, Noblesville, and Westfield. (Photo from the yearbook collection of Olin Edgell.)

Mulford "Muff" Davis spent 15 years coaching at Frankton, where his teams won 139 games. Davis, an Elwood grad, went on to play at the University of Kentucky. He was selected for the Silver Anniversary Team in 1966 and elected to the Indiana Basketball Hall of Fame in 1989. (Photo from the yearbook collection of Olin Edgell.)

The Royerton Redbirds had a perfect regular season for Myron Dickerson in 1961, but they fell in the sectional to Muncie Burris. Eleven seasons later, Dickerson had moved on to Connersville and his Spartan team won the State Championship. Dickerson ended his coaching career with a 380-158 record and was elected to the Indiana Basketball Hall of Fame in 1995. (Photo from the yearbook collection of Olin Edgell.)

Herman Neuenschwander won a regional title with tiny Monroe in 1943 before being called away to help with the war effort. When he returned, he coached the Hartford Township Gorillas to a 1948 sectional championship and an appearance in the final game of the regional. This 1936 Berne graduate had a 140-44 career coaching record. (Photo from the yearbook collection of Olin Edgell.)

Chester Township of Wabash County upset Marion and Kokomo to win a regional in 1948 for Coach Gerald "Doe" Faudree. (Photo from the yearbook collection of Olin Edgell.)

Four

HOOSIER GYMS

The second floor of the Dubach Garage in Lynn Grove was the home floor first for Lynn Grove and later for Hartford Township (Adams County). (Photo from the yearbook collection of Olin Edgell.)

Pleasant Mills coach Gerald Vizard personally called on every voter in St. Mary's Township to get him or her to sign a petition to get a gym built at Pleasant Mills High School. All but two voters in the township signed the petition and construction was started in 1939. (Photo from the yearbook collection of Olin Edgell.)

For a long time the Pleasant Mills gym was thought to have the best basketball court in Adams County. When the gym was being built, the township trustee personally inspected every piece of wood that went into the floor. (Photo from the yearbook collection of Olin Edgell.)

56

This gym at Kentland was the home of the "Blue Devils." (Photo from the collection of Bob Adams.)

The Auburn "Red Devils" called the Alumni gym home. Auburn had a great run in the late 1940s and early 1950s, winning sectional and regional titles in 1945, 1949, 1950, 1951, and 1952. The 1949 team advanced all the way to the final four with Keith Showalter at the helm. (Photo by Bob Adams.)

Want to buy an old school? The old Sandusky High School in Decatur County was for sale in early 2002. It was the home of Ralph Marlow, the Gimble Award winner in 1921. (Photo by Bob Adams.)

This gym at Berne was home to the Bears. It was built in the 1940s and is still in use today as an elementary gym by the South Adams School Corporation. (Photo from the yearbook collection of Olin Edgell.)

The school at Bourbon is long gone, but this gym, which was the home court of the "Comets," is still used by the community. (Photo by Bob Adams.)

This scoreboard was found in the old Bridgeton gym in Parke County. The former home of the Raccoons was later used as a place to exhibit arts and crafts during the Parke County Covered Bridge Festival. (Photo by Bob Adams.)

The Bryant Owls never had a gym to call "home" before this concrete block building was constructed in the early 1950s. Even though the high school is gone, the building is still used by the community and is currently undergoing restoration. (Photo by Bob Adams.)

This building was the home of the Butler "Windmills" and was later the first gym used by the East Side "Blazers." (Photo by Bob Adams.)

Even though it doesn't look like an igloo, this private home was once the home gym of the Chili Polar Bears. (Photo by Bob Adams.)

Chrysler Field house at New Castle has been the home of the Trojans since 1959. It is the largest high school gymnasium in the world. It seats 9,314 people. Indiana is home to 15 of the largest 16 high school gyms in the nation. (Photo by Bob Adams.)

The Wildcats of Clinton High School, who used to play in this gym, now play for South Vermillion, a consolidation of Clinton, Dana, Hillsdale, and St. Bernice. (Photo from the yearbook collection of Olin Edgell.)

Converse High School was torn down decades ago, but this community building still stands in the small Miami town as a living monument to the Converse High School "Bordermen." (Photo by Bob Adams.)

This building began life in the late 1840s as a church in Decatur. It was later bought by Decatur Postmaster John Bosse and turned into an Opera House and skating rink. The Decatur Athletic Boosters leased the building for Decatur High School basketball games, and then bought the building for use by the school in the mid teens. Decatur High School used the building until the new gym at the Decatur Lincoln school building was completed in the mid twenties. Other county schools used the building until Kirkland High School bought the building in 1928, dismantled it, and rebuilt it across the road from the old Kirkland High School. (Photo courtesy of the Adams County Historical Society.)

This shot was taken from the Decatur sectional of 1922, and shows the interior of the Decatur gym. This building was later dismantled and taken six miles west of Decatur and used by Kirkland Township as a gym. (Photo from the yearbook collection of Olin Edgell.)

This is a shot of the same gym after it was moved to Kirkland Township. The Kangaroos had won the sectional in 1928, and as a reward, the gym was built. When Kirkland Township closed at the end of the 1948-1949 school year, the building became the first Adams Central gym, and was used as a home floor by the Greyhounds until the new school at Monroe was completed in 1954. The gym still lives on, only in a different form. When it was auctioned off, a local farmer bought it, and used the building material to build a new house. (Photo from the yearbook collection of Olin Edgell.)

64

This building was used by Economy High School (Wayne County) students as a gym until the school closed and the students were bussed to Hagerstown. (Photo by Bob Adams.)

This was the home of the Freetown Spartans in Jackson County. The building is still used by the community and features a glass backboard at one end and wood backboard at the other. (Photo by Bob Adams.)

The lines on the court at the new Lincoln gym at Decatur hadn't been painted yet when this shot was taken in the mid 1920s. This building was torn down in 1998. (Photo from the yearbook collection of Olin Edgell.)

The WPA funded the project and local labor was used when the Roll gym was built in the 1930s. Roll High School is gone, but the gym still exists in the tiny Blackford County hamlet. (Photo from the yearbook collection of Olin Edgell.)

The Roll "Red Rollers" and this gym were the pride of the community until the school closed in the early 1960s. (Photo from the yearbook collection of Olin Edgell.)

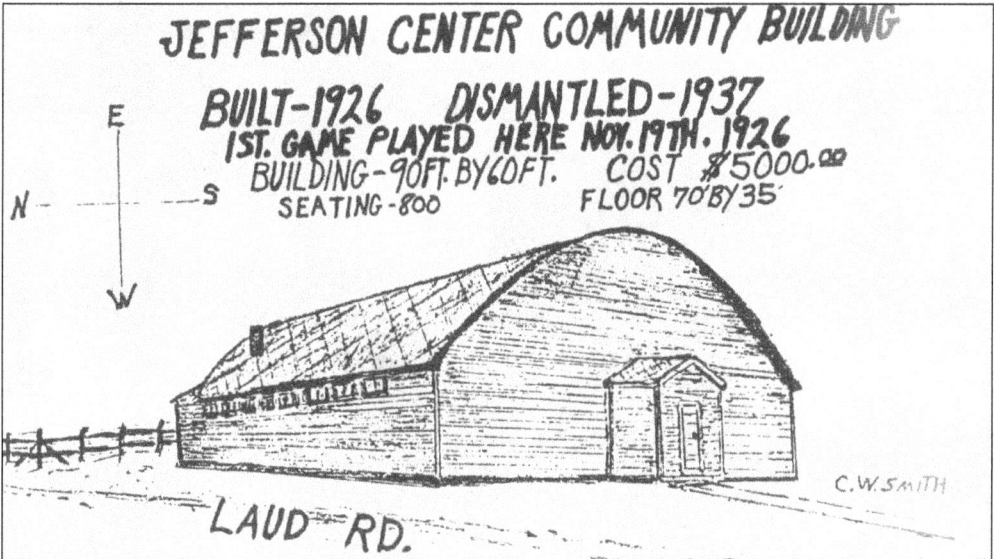

JEFFERSON CENTER COMMUNITY BUILDING
BUILT-1926   DISMANTLED-1937
1ST. GAME PLAYED HERE NOV. 19TH. 1926
BUILDING-90FT. BY 60FT.   COST $5000.00
SEATING-800   FLOOR 70'BY 35'
C.W.SMITH
LAUD RD.

Area residents constructed this building so that the Jefferson Center (Whitley County) Tigers would have a place to play. Built in 1926 at the cost of $5,000, it was dismantled in 1937 when the new gym at the school opened. (Photo from the yearbook collection of Olin Edgell.)

This building in Hagerstown was the long time home of the "Tigers." (Photo by Bob Adams.)

This building, now used as a community center by the people of Michigantown, was once the home of the Michigantown "Ganders" in Clinton County. (Photo from the collection of Bob Adams.)

This building in Lawrenceburg was one of the first homes of the Lawrenceburg basketball teams. (Photo from the yearbook collection of Olin Edgell.)

The Liberty Center Lions were wearing their home (white) uniforms when this picture was taken in 1942. Note the black Converse gym shoes, which were standard foot attire for teams in that era. (Photo from the yearbook collection of Olin Edgell.)

Although this barn now houses livestock and farm equipment, it was once the home of the Little York Wildcats. The backboards are still up in this building in Washington County. (Photo by Bob Adams.)

Jack Butcher, who holds the record (806) for career wins as an Indiana High School basketball coach, played in this Loogootee gym when he played for the Lions. The Lions used this gym, which holds about 300 spectators, until the new school was built in the 1960s. (Photo by Bob Adams.)

ST. JOHN HIGH SCHOOL GYMNASIUM, LOOGOOTEE, INDIANA

For several years, the small Martin County town of Loogootee had two high schools. This building was home to the Loogootee St. John's Eagles. (Photo by Bob Adams.)

Mooresville was proud of its Pioneer basketball team and just as proud of this gym when it was built in the first quarter of the last century. (Photo by Bob Adams.)

This was the long-time home of the Kewanna Indians.

The New Augusta "Red Devils" (Marion County) called this building home before Pike High School was built. (Photo from the collection of Bob Adams.)

This gym in Dubois County was home to the Dubois High School "Jeeps." The nickname didn't come from the popular World War II vehicle, but rather from a character in a Popeye comic book.

Charles Steidle was the coach for the Pendleton Irish, who advanced to the final 16 in 1947. This building was the home court for the Irish. (Photo from the collection of Bob Adams.)

Way back in 1923, Perrysville won their only sectional. The Eagles made it all the way to the "Sweet 16" before bowing out of the tourney. They called this building home. Students from this small Vermillion County town now attend North Vermillion High School. (Photo by Bob Adams.)

Pine Village was well known for its professional football team at the turn of the century. This gym, built in 1940, was home to the Pine Knots, who won six sectional titles before the school closed and merged with West Lebanon and Williamsport to form Seeger High School. (Photo by Bob Adams.)

Quincy is just a spot on the map in Owen County. The Quincy "Aces" entertained area basketball fans in this building before the school closed and the students were sent to Cloverdale. (Photo by Bob Adams.)

The Fort Wayne War Memorial Coliseum was opened in the early 1950s and was host to several sectionals, regionals, and semi-finals. Since the advent of class basketball, the only high school basketball played in the building is the Allen County Athletic Conference Tourney. (From the collection of Bob Adams.)

This old scoreboard was found recently under the bleachers at the old Roll gym in Blackford County. (Photo by Bob Adams.)

This large building can be found in Rushville and is the long-time home of the Rushville Lions. (Photo by Bob Adams.)

The pride of the "Lions," this building in Salem was home to the Salem High School basketball teams in Washington County. (Photo from the collection of Bob Adams.)

Although it is used for storage now, this building in the small Henry County community of Cadiz used to rock on Friday and Saturday night when the "Spaniards" played. (Photo by Bob Adams.)

You don't have to leave Indiana to visit Mexico, Chili, Moscow, or Boston. This gym was the home of the Mexico Bulldogs, and is now used by the small community in Cass County.

Tyson Auditorium in Versailles owes its existence to "Uncle Jim" Tyson. Tyson was a "hobo" printer who ended up in Chicago where he helped a fellow named Walgreen start a drug store chain. Money from this endeavor funded may projects in this Ripley County town. When Milan won the state in 1954, they played their "home" games here and the sectional was also held in this building. (Photo by Bob Adams.)

The "Hatchet House" in Washington has been the long-time home of the Washington Hatchets. The gym seats 7,090 people. Washington has claimed three state championships. (Photo from the collection of Bob Adams.)

All that remains of West Lebanon High School is this gym, the former home of the "Pikers." (Photo by Bob Adams.)

After Wingate won back-to-back state titles in 1913 and 1914, the town folk responded by building this gym in this small Montgomery County community. (Photo by Bob Adams.)

This "Wall of Fame" in the old Heltonville gym honors former Blue Jacket greats.(Photo by Bob Adams.)

This picture shows the exterior of the huge gym at Huntingburg. (Photo by Bob Adams.)

This building, which was built in 1925, was the home of the "Happy Hunters" until the huge new gym was opened in November of 1951. (Photo by Bob Adams.)

While most of the newer schools have fairly generic nicknames (Patriots seems to be a favorite), that wasn't the case before the school consolidation craze of the 1960s. The Tippecanoe Police Dogs and Spencer COPS (Center of Population) were just a couple of teams with unique nicknames. The school at Bedford named their team the "Stonecutters" in honor of the local limestone industry. In the early 1970s, Dennis Quaid and Daniel Stern made a movie called "Breaking Away" which was about the "Little 500" held annually at Indiana University. In the movie, the college kids called the locals "Cutters."

When the town of Oolitic needed a new school for its pupils, the local limestone quarries supplied the material and the WPA supplied the funding and the labor. Dan Bush, who guided Bedford North Lawrence and Damon Bailey to a state title, was a graduate of Oolitc. (Photo from the collection of Bob Adams.)

This gym in Batesville was the home of the Bulldogs before a new school and gym were built just outside of this Ripley County town. (Photo from the collection of Bob Adams.)

Bedford was very proud of the "Stonecutters" and this gym, which is still standing in the county seat of Lawrence County. (Photo from the collection of Bob Adams.)

The Bicknell "Bulldogs" who called this building home now play for North Knox, a consolidation of Bicknell, Bruceville, Edwardsport, Freelandville, Oaktown, Sanborn, and Westphalia. (Photo from the collection of Bob Adams.)

Gaston High School was gutted by fire in the early 1920s. While a new building and gym was being constructed, the students were sent to other schools. The "Bulldogs" played in this building, now used as a community center.

When fire destroyed the Williams High School in the early days of World War II, the "Bulldogs" were sent to Huron High School for a few years until material could be procured and a new school built. Competition between the two schools was so great, that when the Huron school burnt a few years later, the community refused to send their students to the new Williams school. The Huron pupils were educated in local buildings and homes until a new building was completed.

After the old Huron school and gym burned, it was replaced by this structure. The last Beaver graduated from this building in 1963.

The Crawfordsville Athenians used this gym and building for several years before a new school was constructed on the outskirts of this Montgomery County town. (Photo by Bob Adams.)

Gibson County was the home of the Mt. Olympus "Mountaineers," who played their home games in this building. (Photo by Wendell Trogdon.)

Wilkinson High School closed almost four decades ago, and the students now go to Eastern Hancock, but the home of the Bulldogs now houses a hardware store. (Photo by Bob Adams.)

This was the home of the Laconia Aces until 1958. (Photo by Wendell Trogdon.)

This building, built in 1921, was the home of the Berne "Fighting Five," and the Berne "Bears." It was also used by Jefferson Township of Adams County as a home court. It now serves as the Berne Public Library. (Photo from the collection of Bob Adams.)

The "Millers" of Noblesville played their home games in this building for several years. (Photo by Bob Adams.)

This gym, which is attached to the back of the old Lancaster Township High School in Wells County, is slated for demolition soon. Built in 1940, it first served as a home for the "Bobcats," and was later used by the Norwell school system as an elementary school gym. (Photo by Bob Adams.)

The Bridgeton Raccoons played in this gym until they consolidated with Mecca, Montezuma, and Rosedale to form Riverton Parke High School in Parke County. (Photo by Bob Adams.)

This building in Fayette County was first the home of the Harrisburg "Hornets" and later the home of the Fayette Central teams. (Photo by Bob Adams.)

The Lima Orioles used to call this building home in the small LaGrange county town. (Photo by Bob Adams.)

This gym was on the campus of Oakland City College and was the home of both the Oakland City College team as well as the Oakland City High School team, whose nickname was the "Acorns." (Photo from the collection of Bob Adams.)

Before Romney merged with Jackson Township, Shadeland, and West Point to become Southwestern, this gym in Tippecanoe County was the home of the "Pirates." Southwestern High School is long gone also, as it consolidated with Wainwright, (which was a consolidation of Lauramie Township and Dayton), to form McCutcheon High School. Lauramie Township was also an early merger of the high schools at Clarks Hill and Stockwell. (Photo by Bob Adams.)

Now used by the Springville Volunteer Fire Department, this building was once the home of the Springville "Hornets." (Photo by Bob Adams.)

This was the home court of the Millersburg "Millers" in Elkhart County (Photo from the collection of Bob Adams.)

The Winchester Community High School Field house, home of the "Golden Falcons," underwent extensive renovation a couple of years ago. It is located in Randolph County. (Photo by Bob Adams.)

Time and the elements have not been very kind to this building, which was the home of the Richland Township Red Devils. Richland Township was a consolidation of Mellott and Newtown in Fountain County. (Photo by Bob Adams.)

This gym was the home of the Ossian Bears in Wells County. While the Ossian Bears are no more, (they merged with Lancaster Township to become the Norwell Knights), and the school is long gone, this gym is still being used by Ossian Elementary students. (Photo from the yearbook collection of Olin Edgell.)

Jasonville in Greene County was the home of this gym, the home of the "Yellow Jackets." (Photo from collection of Bob Adams.)

The Orland Community Building once was home to the "Tigers." The Orland American Legion now uses it. (Photo from the yearbook collection of Olin Edgell.)

The Gerald Yentes Memorial Gym at Pennville was once the home of the Pennville Bulldogs. It is now used as an elementary school gym. (Photo by Bob Adams.)

The first home of the South Adams "Starfires" was the old Berne High School. The school and this gym were built in the early 1940s. Berne and Geneva consolidated to form South Adams in 1966. This is a picture from the "Starfires'" first season. (Photo from the yearbook collection of Olin Edgell.)

The Merrillville gym was brand spanking new when this picture was taken for the 1928 Merrillville yearbook. (From the collection of Bob Adams.)

This gym in Johnson County was the home court of the Edinburgh "Lancers." (From the collection of Bob Adams.)

A familiar site in Elkhart County, this gym is still standing, a living monument to the New Paris "Cubs." (Photo by Bob Adams.)

Hall of Famer Dave Nicholson played for the Vallonia "Redbirds" in this gym located in Jackson County. He would later coach two undefeated teams at Darlington and be elected president of the Indiana Basketball Hall of Fame. (Photo by Bob Adams.)

This gym in Huntington County was the pride of the small town of Lancaster. Citizens of this village filled this structure on home dates to cheer on their "Lancers." (Photo from the yearbook collection of Olin Edgell.)

Five

CHEERLEADERS, MASCOTS, AND TROPHIES

Edward Todd and Victor Harris led the cheers in 1924 for the Oaklandon "Oaks." (From the collection of Bob Adams.)

Joy Sprunger, Lynn Gillespie, Joan Yager, and Karen Stauffer were the first varsity basketball cheerleaders at South Adams. (Photo from the yearbook collection of Olin Edgell.)

This trio of Bob Johnston, Elizabeth Johnston, and Rex Bovine led the cheers for the Adams Central "Greyhounds" in 1951. (Photo from the yearbook collection of Olin Edgell.)

100

Alice Myers and Betty Wendel exhorted people to cheer for the 1950 Jefferson Township "Warriors." (Photo from the yearbook collection of Olin Edgell.)

Margie Beyl, Wilma Rice, Fay Popp, and Freda Harris provided the spark for the Silver Creek "Dragons" during the 1951-1952 season. (Photo from the yearbook collection of Olin Edgell.)

Leading the cheers for the Bippus "Tigers" in 1957 were Jean Smith, Marge Wolhford, and Judy Lancaster. (Photo from the yearbook collection of Olin Edgell.)

Joan Jarrett, Roberta Garton, and Norma Mann provided the instruction for the Liberty Center cheer block in 1942. (Photo from the yearbook collection of Olin Edgell.)

The Berne basketball team gave this cheer block a lot to yell about in 1957. (Photo from the yearbook collection of Olin Edgell.)

Bill Bell and Ruth Engle exhibited their school spirit for Decatur in 1925. (Photo from the yearbook collection of Olin Edgell.)

This fierce "Redbird" brought fear to the hearts of many of the Royerton foes. (Photo from the yearbook collection of Bob Adams)

The Limberlost Bell was the championship trophy of the Adams County Tourney. It was named after the home of Gene Stratton Porter, a famous author who made her home for a time in Geneva. Her home was named after the Limberlost Swamp, which covered a large area between Geneva and Bryant. Geneva possessed the Bell in 1959, seen here surrounded by Cardinal cheerleaders Roxie Bauman, Linda Wilhoite, Janet Laux, and Janice Van Emaon. (Photo from the yearbook collection of Olin Edgell.)

The Roll Red Roller was built by Roll shop students following Roll's sectional championship in 1951. It was designed to fit over a child's tricycle. A small child would be put inside the Roller to ride around the floor during breaks in the action. (Photo supplied by Olin Edgell.)

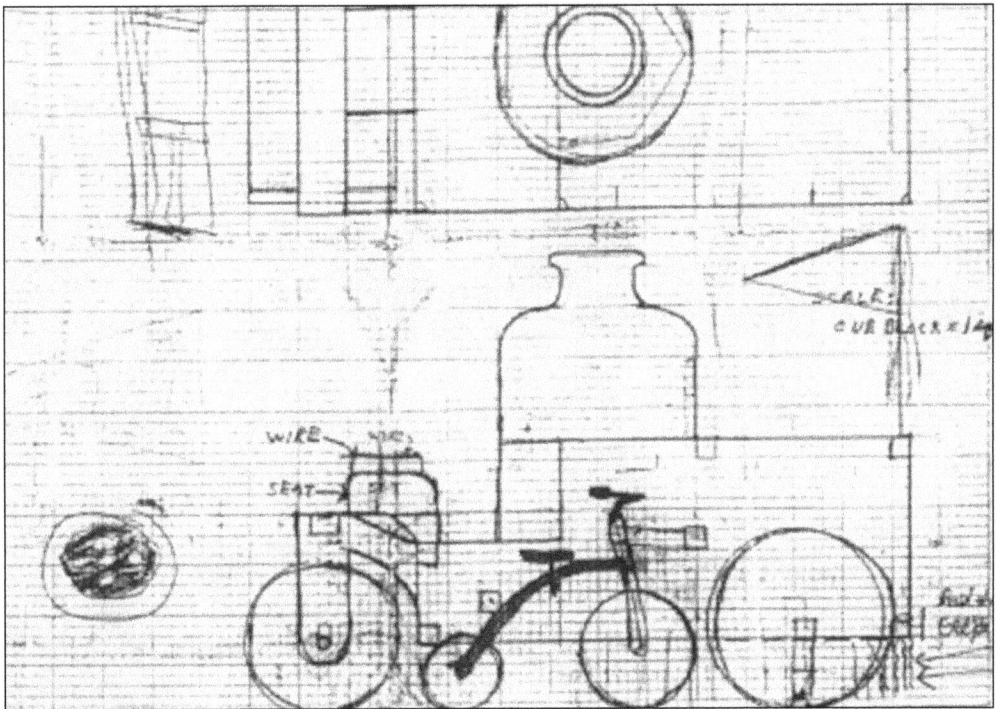

This is the plan the students drew up and used to build the Roll Red Roller. (Photo supplied by Olin Edgell.)

Sandra George, Sue Ritchison, and Ada Ritter led the cheers for the "Hilltoppers" at Needmore High School in 1950. (Photo from the yearbook collection of Olin Edgell.)

The cheerleaders for the Fishers "Tigers" in 1958 were Nancy West, Susan Wolfe, Sondra Hanks, and Doris Farr. (Photo from the yearbook collection of Olin Edgell.)

Senior cords were popular in the 1950s and 1960s. The seniors in the cheer block would buy a pair of white or light beige corduroy pants and then have their friends sign them. They would then wear them to all home games. This picture is from Fillmore High School in 1967. (Photo from the yearbook collection of Olin Edgell.)

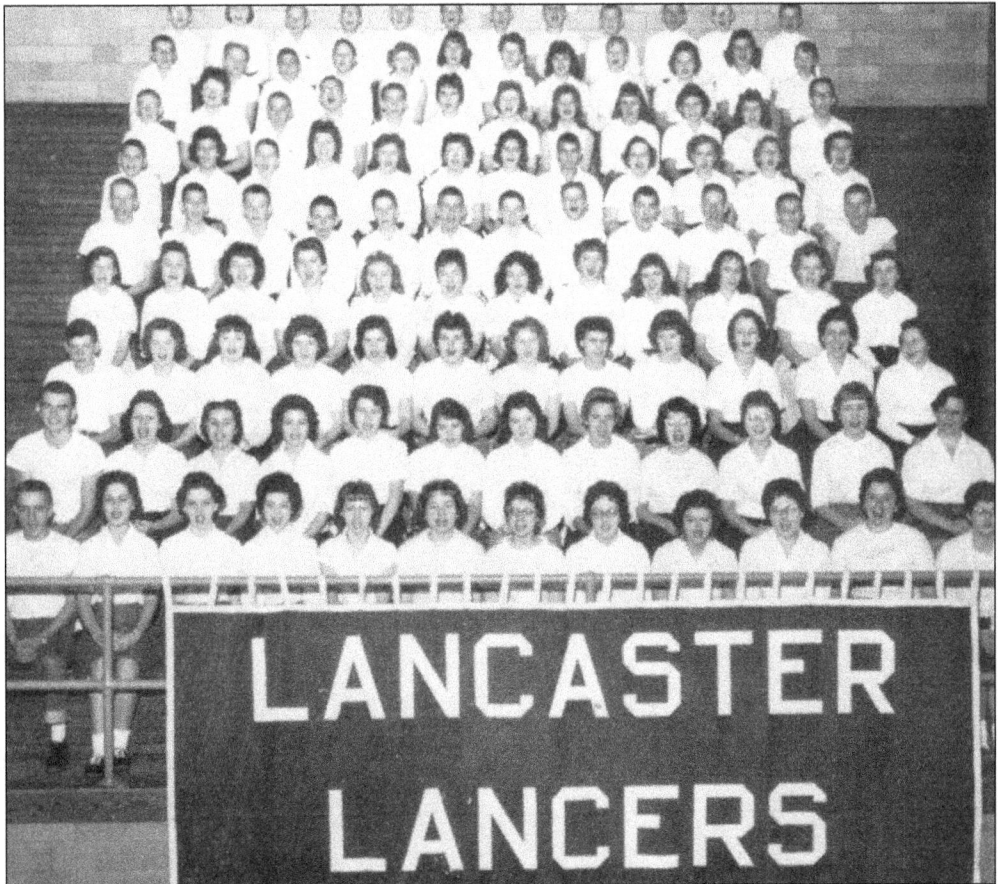

Practically every girl at Lancaster Central in Huntington County was a member of the "Lancer" cheer block. (Photo from the yearbook collection of Olin Edgell.)

Payne (left) and Sanq (below) were cheerleaders for Brazil in the early 1920s. One of their cheers was: Terrio Rex, Terrio Rex, Hallu, Buzzu, Buzza, Bussex, We're the members of B.H.S., Jason, Jason, A Ha. Zip, Sow, Wow, Wow, Tiger, Tiger, Woooooooo. (Photo from the collection of Bob Adams.)

"SANQ"

Sanq, the other Brazil cheerleader. (Photo from the collection of Bob Adams.)

With a school on a lake, and a nickname like the Marines, is it any wonder these 1940 Hamilton cheerleaders dressed like sailors? (Photo from the collection of Bob Adams.)

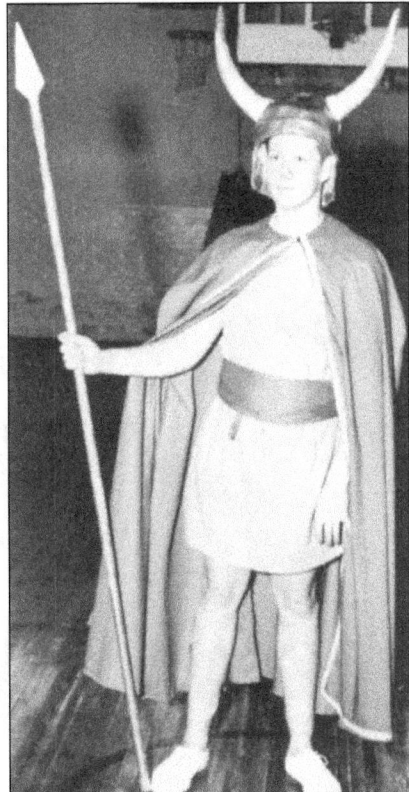

Brian Hubert was the last Eaton Norseman before the school closed in 1967. (Photo from the collection of Bob Adams.)

Linda Riley and Beverly Myers cheered for the Pleasant Mills "Spartans" in 1961. (Photo from the yearbook collection of Olin Edgell.)

These 1944 Williamsport cheerleaders were Joyce Zenor, Richard Fix, and Betty DeBord-Hurley (Yea! Rah! Bingy!). (Photo from the yearbook collection of Olin Edgell.)

110

The cheerleading of Jerry West, Claudia Drayer, Rita Marsh, Chuck Vise and Norma Vise led the Yorktown "Tigers" to a Delaware County championship in 1954. (Photo from the yearbook collection of Bob Adams.)

Carl Sheets, Katie Hower, and Marion Baker led cheers for the Decatur "Yellow Jackets."

Marie Bennett, Brenda Walker, Lana Little, Linda Faust, Elaine Twitchell, Karen Faust, and Linda Clauson led the cheers as the Linden Bulldogs won the 1964 Montgomery County tourney. (Photo from the collection of Bob Adams.)

Kermit Purcell and Edgar Young led the cheers for the Crawfordsville Athenians in 1930. (Photo from the collection of Bob Adams.)

Six

THEY'RE GONNA PUT ME IN THE MOVIES

The citizens of the small Lawrence County town of Heltonville honored their favorite son, Damon Bailey, by erecting this monument. Bailey set the all-time career scoring record in the state with 3,134 points. Heltonville is also the hometown of well-known author Wendell Trogdon. (Photo by Bob Adams.)

David Anspaugh was better known in high school as the quarterback of the football team and the point guard for the Decatur Yellow Jackets. A couple of decades later, he would direct a little movie about Indiana High School basketball called *Hoosiers*. (From the yearbook collection of Olin Edgell.)

Nineveh High School in Johnson County was reborn as "Hickory High School" in the movie *Hoosiers*. This building burned down a few years ago. (From the collection of Bob Adams.)

114

Thanks to that old Hollywood magic, the old Knightstown gym in Henry County was turned into the home court of the Hickory "Huskers" in the movie *Hoosiers*. (Photo by Bob Adams.)

Although the outside of this gym was never seen in the movie, the old Lebanon gym was given new life as the Jasper gym in the movie *Hoosiers*. (Photo by Bob Adams.)

Probably the most photographed water tower in the world, the Milan water tower honors the 1954 Milan Indians, who won the state championship that season with a 32-30 win over Muncie Central. The movie *Hoosiers* was based on the 1954 Milan win. (Photo by Bob Adams.)

Case Arena, on the campus of Frankfort High School, became the "Western Field house" in the movie *Blue Chips*. The movie starred Nick Nolte as the coach, and Bob Knight, the former Indiana University coach, had a role as a (surprise) coach. (Photo by Bob Adams.)

Baseball great Gil Hodges was an alumnus of Petersburg High School. (From the collection of Bob Adams.)

Sportscasting legend Chris Schenkel graduated from Bippus High School in Huntington County. Sandy Thompson, a Fort Wayne TV weather person, also went to this small school. (Photo from the yearbook collection of Olin Edgell.)

Fairmount High School in Grant County can count movie star James Dean and cartoonist Jim Davis among its graduates. Dean was a starting guard for the "Quakers" in the late 1940s. (Photo by Bob Adams.)

Bob Plump, who hit the game winning shot in the 1954 state championship game for Milan, now owns a restaurant in Broad Ripple called "Plump's Last Shot." He was recently the subject of a book called: *The Last of the Small Town Heroes.* (Photo by Terri Adams.)

Some 40,000 fans saw Damon Bailey lead his Bedford North Lawrence Stars to a 1990 state championship with a win over Concord in the Hoosier (now RCA) Dome. It was the largest crowd ever to see a high school basketball game. Bailey is the all-time leading scorer in the state with 3,134 points. He was the subject of at least two books, *Shooting Stars*, and *Damon, Living a Dream*. He went on to a college career at Indiana University and played professionally for a number of years before retiring. (Photo by Wendell Trogdon.)

Shanna Zolman of Wawasee High School led the state in scoring four straight years, and is the only girls' player in the state to score more than 3,000 career points. She ended her career with 3,085 points, and will continue her playing career at Tennessee. She was the subject of articles in several national publications, including *Sports Illustrated* and *USA Today*. (Photo by Shane Frost.)

The most famous team to come out of Indiana was this 1954 Milan team, which upset much larger Muncie Central in 1954, 32-30, on a last second shot by Bobby Plump. Plump (#25) also won the Trester Award that season. The movie *Hoosiers* was based on the exploits of this team.

The Indiana Basketball Hall of Fame is the only high school sports hall of fame in the nation. Then Vice-President Dan Quayle, a Huntington native, was present when this building was opened. The Hall of Fame is located in New Castle. (Photo by Bob Adams.)

Seven

WHAT HAPPENED TO THE OLD SCHOOLS?

When the township trustee tried to force Onward High School to consolidate with another local school, the citizens of this small Cass County town surrounded the building and refused to let him in. When he came back with a contingent of state police, about 200 people armed with shotguns met them. The trustee cut off funding to the school, but the locals kept it open with fund drives, chicken barbeques, and car washes. The state eventually took away the schools accreditation and the school was force to close. (Photo by Bob Adams.)

Jack Meyer, second from the left in the back row, was the first 1,000 point career scorer in Adams County. Meyer played for Hartford Township High School in Adams County. He ended his career with 1,023 points after scoring 25 points in his final game, a sectional-final loss to Decatur. His granddaughter, Amy, also scored over 1,000 career points while playing for South Adams. Head coach Herman Neuenschwander, (all the way to the right in row 2), won sectional titles at both Hartford Township and Monroe. (Photo from the yearbook collection of Olin Edgell.)

By 1963, Hartford Township High School was closed and its students dispersed to Geneva and Berne. These two schools later merged to form South Adams High School. (Photo supplied by Olin Edgell.)

122

Homer Stonebraker led Wingate to back-to-back state titles in the early years of the century. Wingate High School was closed in 1953 and consolidated with New Richmond to form Coal Creek Central. This school, pictured above, did not last too long, as it merged with Bowers, Darlington, Linden, and Waynetown to form North Montgomery High School. (Photo by Bob Adams.)

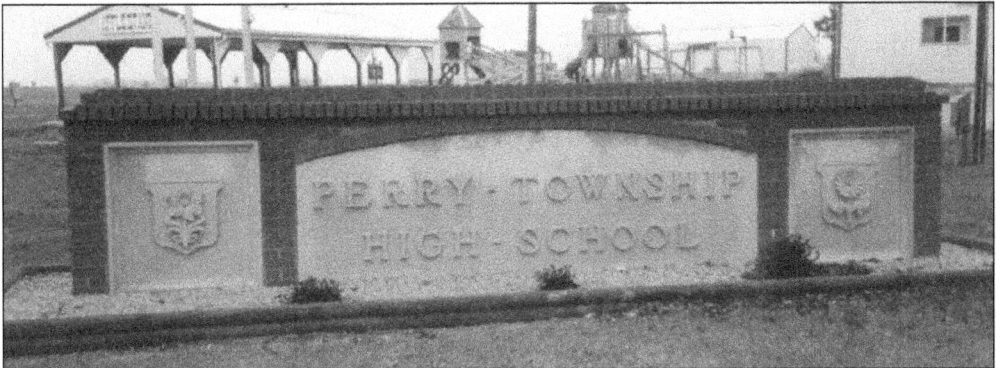

This stone once graced the entrance of Cory High School. Now this monument is all that is left of the home of the "Apple Boys." (Photo by Bob Adams.)

The home floor of the Kitchel "Cowboys" is still used by the townsfolk, but Kitchel High School has long since been torn down. While the "Cowboys" are no more, this marker honors their two sectional championship teams. (Photo by Bob Adams.)

Not many people remember when this building was a school. It hasn't housed a high school for almost 80 years. It was the home of the Moscow "River Rats." The "River Rats" were named after the Flat Rock River, which wound through the town. (Photo by Bob Adams.)

124

New Waverly in Cass County was home to this small high school. The school closed in 1959 and the students first were sent to Washington Township, then to the new Lewis Cass consolidation. (Photo supplied by Gene Parks.)

The old school building at New Waverly still stands, but its roof has caved in and there are trees growing in the space that students used to occupy. The building, once the pride of this small Cass County town, is now almost totally hidden by trees and surrounded by a junkyard. (Photo by Bob Adams.)

The town of Raleigh in Rush County once had a team named the "Sir Raleighs." All that remains of the school is this stone, and part of the bell tower. (Photo by Bob Adams.)

The Rockfield Indians used to call this building in Carroll County home. The high school closed in 1949 and the students were first shipped to Camden, then to Delphi. (Photo by Bob Adams.)

This used to be the home of the Raub Ramblers. This was once one of the smallest high schools in the state. The Ramblers were in and out of the state tourney several times because some years they did not have enough boys in the high school to put together a basketball team. The high school closed in 1961, and the students, even though they live in Benton County, attend South Newton High School in Newton County. (Photo by Bob Adams.)

The former home of the Guilford "Wildcats" now is home to the township's volunteer fire department. (Photo by Bob Adams.)

Milltown High School was closed in 1976 and the students were sent to the new Crawford County High School. The home of the "Millers" was torn down shortly afterwards. (From the collection of Bob Adams.)

HIGH SCHOOL BUILDING AMBOY, IND.

Amboy lost this high school building to a fire in 1945. It spelled the end of the Amboy "Pirates." The school was never rebuilt and the students were dispersed to other area schools. (From the collection of Bob Adams.)